Personal Poetry
By
Nicholas James Zornow

Personal Poetry

Nicholas James Zornow

Published by Nicholas James Zornow, 2023.

While every precaution has been taken in the preparation of this book, the publisher assumes no responsibility for errors or omissions, or for damages resulting from the use of the information contained herein.

PERSONAL POETRY

First edition. November 26, 2023.

ISBN: 979-8223362142

Written by Nicholas James Zornow.

Also by Nicholas James Zornow

Beneath The Secret Oak Tree
Midnight Fright Fest
Personal Poetry
They'll All Fall Down
The Ultimate Steal
Me, Not Being Me
A Conversation With Myself
Silently Violent
From My Shallow Beating Heart
Three Of Me
Untitled
The Untold Stories Of...
Mr. C
The Cloud Of Christmas Day
Life With Love
Heartbeats
A Trip To The Devil's Hole
Everything Will Be Alright In The Morning
Populate
Tales from Nick
Red Rose Promise

Watch for more at www.books2read.com/njz.

Table of Contents

"We all go a little mad sometimes"

A.P.

The following are a collection of my personal poems. I know that's already explained in the title. Just know, I don't write poetry often but when I do, it is a journal of my heart.

Enjoy!

Acceptance

I feel so alone
    In a world of judgment
I just want to fit in
In this life of worthlessness
Can I find someone
Someone who accepts
Me for me
Or am I just one of the many lonely
Please like me
Please love me
Because I need others
Everybody needs somebody
And I'm just one
One of the many
One just wanting friendship
One just needing love
One who can't bear to die alone
I am scared
I am afraid
Give me a reason not to be
And I will feel free

Panic

Holding my breath
    My heart pumps fast
Unable to speak
Panic
Crippled beyond belief
Life gives no relief
I want to live
I want to go
Break the barrier
And see where life takes me
But panic
Panic is a daily struggle
Regain courage
Regain strength
That is what I must do
Patience and resilience
Panic's enemies
I will use them to defeat panic
And establish self-dominance
Which will bring inner peace
Because panic
Must be destroyed.

Hatred

Damage is done
        You brought hurt on me
No excuse will do
The sight of you makes me turn
It makes the trauma burn
Why did you hate me
When I begged for you to love me
Love is gone
It never existed
I look at faces
And I see you
I see evil
I was innocent
You were vicious
I will move on from hatred
But it will take time
Time I have plenty
So I will be patient
And let the hatred disintegrate
Into nothing
Nothing
Just like you

Self-belief

I've never believed in myself
    I still don't
I still wont
Until I prove myself wrong
I try not to fail
the more I try
The deeper I sink
Please don't let life
Take me away
Without proving to myself
That I'm okay
Okay the way I am
On the out
And within

Jason

I held you
   We made eye contact
Innocence in your face
I will never forget
You were taken
Taken too soon
I love you so much
And don't know what to do
Nephew named Jason
Will always be in my heart
My mind
And will never leave
I'm the Uncle you don't know
But know this
The unknown uncle
Loves you more than any
Any uncle that you could dream of
Ill always be here
If you want to know me
Love
You have shown me
Love

Will always be here for you

Chloe

I have dreams
    Wishing I had held you
Wishing I had known you
I carry your picture with me
Always
Niece names Chloe
With eyes like the clear ocean
My heart aches
Missing you and your brother
Forever like no other
If I ever get to meet you
I will share
Share anything you want to know
I am an open book
Written inside
I love you

Dad

I t scares me to think about
		Life without you
I love you so much
Through and through
You taught me how to work hard
I hope I made you proud
But there is more life to come
For you and me to spend together
Father and son
No matter what's done
Me and my dad
Couldn't make me more glad
I am grateful for all
You speak seldom
But what you do say stands tall
I love you always
Father and son

Mom

You are constant and consistent
　　You brought me life
You gave me love
I gave back
I hope you feel that I did so
Because how much I love you
You don't even know
We have a bond
That will never be broken
We laugh
Without one word spoken
You are my life
I'd do anything
Anything to make you smile
Because
Don't forget
Ill be here for a while
With you
Side by side
I love you

Silence

Silence brings out the worst in me
    That is when the demons wake
In the silence
I become mad
In the silence
I become sad
Quiet tear drops fall on the floor
In this dreadful silence
I wait impatiently
To hear a voice again
But I am alone
And the silence is my only company

Trust

Trust
     How do I do so
I am vulnerable
Eager to get out there
But
Trust is what holds me
From happiness
I need to know
That you can keep a secret
The obvious secret is that
Trust is for oblivions

Normal

I've been told
　　I'm normal
But I do not act
Nor do I feel normal
Is normal good
Is normal bad
I believe it is a state of mind
If you say you are normal
Then you are so
If you believe you are not
You shall not be
Normality in its purest form
Is being yourself
At all costs
Not caring what others think
Individuality in unique
Unique is being yourself
So
In essence
Being unique to yourself
Is the definition of normality
Everyone is normal

But
There is no such thing as normal
There is only
You

Apocalypse

Fall in line
    Because the world is about to end
Fall in line
Because you are next
The beasts of the underworld
Have taken over
Evil has prevailed
A world without good deeds
Becomes corrupt
And that leaves room
For dominance by the monsters
The end is now
Cover your eyes
Its not a pretty sight
Cover your eyes
So you don't see the world's demise

Pray

P ray
What's the point
I ask for help
But never receive
I need guidance
So I wont look for myth
I look to my loved ones for help
Because prayer
Has brought nothing but false hope

Pendulum

B ack and forth
      Swinging with purpose
Tell others when it is time
Left to right
You sway
Silently moving air around
Moving side to side
Tell us when to do
Do what we need
Timekeeper
Tell us
Please

We

We sit
      And suffer in silence
Waiting for the pain to go away
But it doesn't
So
We plaster on a fake smile
Pretending we're okay
But we're not
All we can do
Is wait
And hope
That we find each other
And fight this together united as one

Tears of blood

With a heavy sigh
I cry
I cry hard with tears of blood
The blood drips onto the floor
Forming a puddle
I am crying so hard
that what I feel on the inside
hurt
in projecting
my tears of blood
they represent
each one
a year in which have suffered
my whole life is suffer
I sulk with this puddle of blood
Until all of the blood in my system
Is now out there
Like the heart that I wear on my sleeve
That is how I began to bleed
In the first place
Vulnerability kills
And

It has killed me

?

I live in the past
     I hate the present
And I dread the future
What is next for me
I don't know
Give me reasons
Give me hope
Give me the tools
On how to cope
Because I can't take another day
The way I'm living now
Misery

Feel

Feelings of dread
    Inside my head
I look to the sky
And it turns blood red
Feelings of nothing at all
Except that ill fail and fall
I don't know how I feel
When will hope reveal
I feel it's never coming
So internally I'm numbing
But I still feel in my dreams
Things are not what they seem
Let me feel something good and new
Because as of right now I'm through
I give up because I cant take it
Unfortunately life is what you make it
I feel less and less
Life is meaningless

Fight

You have to fight
    For your right
Every day
For your sanity
In a world that gives you nothing
I cant help but continue my fussing
Fight
I have none left
Do I have fight in me
Because I do not feel blessed
Fighting takes so much out of me
Let there be peace
So I may be free

Chaos

Chaos stirs in my mind
    Peace I can not find
Chaos continues in my brain
Nothing left but pain
Chaos has reigned supreme
Nothing is what it seems
When chaos takes over
Chaos is the closer

Laughter

Laughing hysterically
        But nothing is funny
Losing my mind
In this battle against life
I continue to laugh
And spread concern
But no one cares
Laughter is infectious when things are funny
But laughter for no reason except hurt
Makes you simply mad
Mad as insane
I have lost my mind
During this laughter

Love

I have no love to write to
    I have no love at all
I long for it
I need it
But life gives me nothing
Love is in the air
But not for me
Love
Is not in this story
The end
The end of my of my story
Loveless

Dare

I dare you to jump
    Take a leap
Get the hell out of your seat
Because the world
Is waiting
Waiting outside
For you

Tumor

E ating it's prey
     Like a stray
Death is in you
Let this death bring you to be alerted
All will end soon
It cant be adverted

Friendship

T he word that is written
    Is a lie
There is no such thing as friendship
So
As I wait for a true friend
I cower and am leery
But there it is
Hidden in plain sight
When you finally agree to trust

Success

I never thought
    That I would make it come true
I write and write
The whole night through
Until I waken to see my dream
Be printed on paper
For all to read
For all to enjoy
I am now a hero
To my younger self
As I am now what I've dreamed of
Something

Violence

I used to be dangerous
    But to only one person
Until I grew restraint
Whatever has bothered me
Whoever has bothered me
Can now relax
As can I
Because I am docile

Cousins

On occasion I think about you
But you're not worth my time
I drew the line
That had to be drawn
You are no longer in my worries
Because I know I'm better
Better than you try to be
You can't reach my level of success
Because it is inside of me
The burning fire of hatred and spite
Keeps me going

Death

D eath
      A slice of the beginning
The beginning of all the hurt
The hurt that will come
When you're the only one
Who's left
Just you and death

Rocking Chair

Movement without progression
        Without reason and without purpose
You sit and rock
But you will never reach your destination

Time

Sometimes seconds go by
    Faster than we could have thought
Minutes tick away slower and slower
Hours turn to days
And not much more after that
Because you have no sense of time
Maybe you ran out

Sound

The sounds of all the earth
     Seems to be piercing my ears
I can't plug them
Because sound overwhelms me
And brings out fear
Pure irrational fear

Betrayal

The consistent fear
    Of no love
It is real
I am proof
I fear love
Because I've never felt it
But
If I do
The person will turn
Turn to hate me
Just as all the others do

Words

I use trickery ways
     In my style of writing
     Placing words in just the perfect spot
     I must not fail and I will not fail
     Because I have the power of words

Heroes

I look left
   I look right
But I see nothing
Or shall I say
No one
No one to call my hero
They exist for some
Not all
As my tears begin to fall
And they won't stop
Not even for a hero

Luck

The scarce moments
    That you think will make change
Leads to not much at all
Except false hope

Cliff

I am hanging on
    But only by one hand
As my grip loosens
I realize I must face it
I must face fear
Me and me alone
Is what it will take
To keep hanging on

Shame

Those feelings
    Of not being good enough
Being embarrassed
I have brought this
This shame
With me day after day
When will I live it down
When the others approve

Wisdom

Wisdom comes with age
And experience
But wisdom does not come to all
Look at the bodies fall
Fall into failure
For lack of wisdom

Goodbye

G oodbye
     Not goodnight
Because we will never know
If the morning will come
When we open our eyes from a slumber
And realize
Nothing is there
Life's final goodbye

The End... for now

Thank you to all readers

Don't miss out!

Visit the website below and you can sign up to receive emails whenever Nicholas James Zornow publishes a new book. There's no charge and no obligation.

https://books2read.com/r/B-A-JBNX-RZDRC

BOOKS 2 READ

Connecting independent readers to independent writers.

Did you love *Personal Poetry*? Then you should read *They'll All Fall Down*[1] by Nicholas James Zornow!

They'll All Fall Down

Written by

Nicholas James Zornow

[2]

A tragic event alters the life of a loving husband and father. Revenge was on his mind and nobody could imagine that hurt would turn to hatred, murder and even the black arts of voodoo. Read more at www.books2read.com/njz.

---

1. https://books2read.com/u/3GovRp

2. https://books2read.com/u/3GovRp

Also by Nicholas James Zornow

Beneath The Secret Oak Tree
Midnight Fright Fest
Personal Poetry
They'll All Fall Down
The Ultimate Steal
Me, Not Being Me
A Conversation With Myself
Silently Violent
From My Shallow Beating Heart
Three Of Me
Untitled
The Untold Stories Of...
Mr. C
The Cloud Of Christmas Day
Life With Love
Heartbeats
A Trip To The Devil's Hole
Everything Will Be Alright In The Morning
Populate
Tales from Nick
Red Rose Promise

Watch for more at www.books2read.com/njz.

About the Author

Nicholas James Zornow is an author from upstate New York. He has many stories available all over the world. His influences are authors like Edgar Allan Poe, Ambrose Bierce, Stephen King and H.G. Wells. He loves writing and aspires to be just as great as the authors he looks up to.

Read more at www.books2read.com/njz.